# Leavings
# From My Table

*poems by*

# Charlene Stegman Moskal

*Finishing Line Press*
Georgetown, Kentucky

# Leavings
# From My Table

## ACKNOWLEDGMENTS

Thank you to all the editors who have published my work in your anthologies,
magazines and online:

After, Time and Tide in chapbook, *One Bare Foot*, Zeitgeist Press
None of Us  in *Helen: A Literary Magazine*
Permanence  in *Dash*
Nightgowns in *Good Works Review*
Valley of Fire  in *Sandstone & Silver; an Anthology of Nevada Poets*
Wall  published in *Exposition Review*
Heart  in *Pomme Journal/Petite Pomme*
Ash in *Sky Island Journal*
Cavity in *Flying Ketchup Review*
Lucky in *The Silent World in Her vase*
Just Not Like This in *Months to Years*
The Closet in *Last Leaves Literary Journal*

Thank you also to Bruce Isaacson, Vogue Robinson and Heather Lang Cassera, Poet
Laureates of Clark County, Nevada and to the poets and writers of the Las Vegas
community whose words inspire and encourage mine.

And to my family and friends whose love supports me in all my endeavors.

*Disclaimer: In some poems small revisions have been made which do not alter the
intent of the poem.*

Publisher: Leah Huete de Maines
Editor: Christen Kincaid
Cover Art: Charlene Stegman Moskal
Author Photo: Barnett O'Hara
Cover Design: Elizabeth Maines McCleavy


Order online: www.finishinglinepress.com
also available on amazon.com

Author inquiries and mail orders:
Finishing Line Press
PO Box 1626
Georgetown, Kentucky 40324
USA

# Table of Contents

# Wall

All the neurotic pieces that hung marionette-like on nerve strings, on loose raw tendons, came together when there was you and formed me solid; a concrete cinder block wall. Some say you know it is right when the wall comes down. I knew it was right when the wall went up; fierce, protective. Love with hearts and flowers superimposed over the past. I was insulated by structure and hope. I was written on by your graffiti with murals of heroes, savages and saviors all of them wearing your face and mine. In the background Tina is singing, *What's love got to do with it?* and I answer, Everything.

## Space Available

There is space available between the roots
of gnarled trees, twisted limbs in old olive groves;
in the margins and the lines between the lines;
in beats between breaths.

A seat is unoccupied in waiting room
plastic chairs with jazz music piped in softly
as buttered white bread for a Sunday breakfast
for me and the dogs.

Pin-hole lapses bridge the air between motes of
dust in beams dancing away from frayed curtains,
casting traces of patterns against pale walls
like old dried rain drops.

Broken gaps span splintered wood of trestle tracks
over ravines splashing white water rapids
wild as water nymphs who wait with open arms
as the cracks claim you

There is space available in the places
where memories are selective for love's sake—
in the empty passenger seat of my car
that bears your shadow.

# Drowning

There's a hairline crack
in the bone of my heart;

that place hard by nature, protective
where calcified memories are stored.
.

It has developed a weakness,
ready to split open when pressured,

turn pericardial fluid into salt tears
and drown the chambers, drench my throat,

fill my mouth in a torrent of No's,
spew a clay slurry that holds the handprint

of your essence to dry in the image
of whom you were and always will be.

## Coo

We sit on a branch;

a quarrel of sparrows,
an unkindness of ravens,
perhaps a single solitary bird
whose mate flew too high,

bumped its head on clouds,
whose feathers now decorate
a crown of suffering, quiet, soft,
cold as the first grey day of winter.

I am the mourning dove.

Struck when least expected,
I limp along a ground
of uneven promises, shards of glass,
search for sustenance in weeds.

From branch to rooftop to gutter,
I grasp for morsels in other's lives,
watch for dangers that veer too close,
try to remember how to coo.

## Key

What if you had found the lock rusted with age,
clogged with dried leaves,
remnants of spider's webs,
twigs of abandoned birds' nests?
What if the key you thought would fit
wasn't the right key at all?
Would you have taken a hammer,
a wedge,
an iron crowbar,
tried to break in to save me?
Or would you have shrugged, walked away,
say you had been given the wrong key
and left it at that?

## Cento for Gene

I am waiting for my number to be called
Rumi said it…… the price of life is a kiss
I was perfectly happy sinking into the depths of you
Barefoot we all walk the glass covered path together
You stepped out of the body, unzipped it like a coat
Tears the crystal rags, viscous tatters of a worn-through soul
Nothing escapes in a house with white walls
And then you closed the shutters on my words
And the house was dark.
Not all poems are written.

**I've had it**


with stroking foreheads
closing lids
mouthing prayers like fairy tales
saying good bye.

with filling up on death
standing strong against tempests
watching a friend rise into my dark skies
knowing tomorrow won't come.

with keeping it to myself,
holding my back to the closing door
choking on the memory of our journey
unable to look in his eyes.

with keening behind closed lips
while I search for strength
to open my anger to sharp winds
forceful enough to carry my grief away.

## Cavity

Memory stands in to fill a hole where he used to be.
My empty palm is a cavity.
It's not like there was always something to fill it,
but when filled it would warm me.
Without a hand in that small space
I am always cold.

## None of Us

He said:

"None of us are the sun.

Arrogance to believe
I am anyone's light
and if I should go out
you would falter, be abandoned,
become dark matter absorbed
by pain, longing, confusion,
self-retribution and fear,
loathe to believe I've been shut off
by some celestial Tesla.

None of us are the sun.

You will not vanish.
Your path will not devolve,
only wobble,
lost in space for a while
until you find a stronger gravity
than love to stabilize
the orbit of your heart.

None of us are the sun"

## You'd Rather Not

There was a breach, a gap, as if you'd rather
not had to acknowledge that part of me,
rather have had the "under-the-surface" me
stay hidden, no stains, no laundry aired.

Maybe my words opened hidden portals,
or maybe you just didn't want to know,
didn't want to feel incapable of lifting the weight.

You were right. It was my problem,
my onus to embrace, explore, expose.
I should not have imposed that on you.
I should not have expected you to carry me,

except in the smiling snapshot kept in your wallet,
the one taken out from time to time to reassure
that that me would always be there.

## Framed

Stopped wings spread,
forever  pinned;
they will do no flying tonight.

Delicate behind glass walls
they fall apart
one wing at a time

imprisoned, stuck
caught in a frame
dusty with age.

Escape is not an option,
hasn't been since the net
was cast mid-flight.

Stilled because of beauty.
There are no winds
to carry them.

Protected, they do not fade
only grow brittle in death
and dry eyed—

a pale imitation of time
not unlike the passage of memory
borne fluttering in dreams.

## Fathers

I investigated you.
I now can put a face to your father.

I no longer need to imagine you
old, weakened, his doppelganger.

I can see his face in yours;
the puckish look you carry.

I can now imagine him
small and weak, lying on his side.

I can see how he is curled;
you said, "like a puppy."

He is no longer
a pale image of you.

I no longer need to substitute
my father's face for his.

And he is nothing like my father
who died lying straight, but shriveled,

dry skinned in his own bed
with Mother by his side.

## Each Time

I never saw you as old
no more than one would see
the ocean as old or weak
deny its immutable power

renewed each time

a wave licks the shore
or crashes ecstatic into it
like a child naked outside
in a summer downpour

renewed each time

the green-white foam is sucked out
and comes racing back
as if it had forgotten something
that's how you were to me

renewed each time

you were gripped
by those inconveniences
that sucked you out from our bed
landed you in sterile rooms

renewed each time

I always thought you would return
as if the tides in your blood
had to rush back to find me
waiting on the shore

renewed each time.

## Nightgowns

Even after he was gone,
the inevitable was a foreign language.

She continued to wear silk nightgowns,
fine lace at the décolleté

that waited till the end of day
to be filled
with remembered        nights

when she would lay next to him
all of him        still intact

with arms that could wrap around
and        two legs

that would slide between hers
and        disturb the sheets.

Now she doesn't move till morning;
the blankets tucked in        tight

Only a shadow says
she has slept there.

**Heart**

When we slept facing each other
our knees met;
your left one, my right.
They formed a cartoon heart.
With our heads close together,
necks stretched towards a kiss
we completed the shape of love.
In the middle there were
only dampened sheets.

## Lucky

We were a pair, he and I. We sat naked by the pool and said, *Boy, are we lucky.* His skin was softer than mine, tenderized by age, it had few muscles to cling to. It was two sizes too large.

Flesh cascaded in lava flows from chest to belly to pubis; crenellated along the upper edge of his thigh to the bottom of his buttocks. He saw himself in the mirror but not in my eyes. Only now can I acknowledge what he saw. I find imperfections that emerge overnight like strawberry plants that spread rhizomes in my skin, my muscles, my flesh. Where once I was smooth supple suede I am now dry riverbed, alligatored. I do not recognize my shape in the mirror. She is a "bruja" who by magic inhabits my body. He hid it well, said I was beautiful but I heard his voice wanting it to be true. And so we sat naked by the pool unembarrassed and ignored the changes, reassured each other and said, *Boy, are we lucky.*

## Time and Tide

I was aware as I held you,
that I was a tentacle,
suckers at the ready
to cling to you as a rock
under fathoms of time.

But you,

made strong by skeletons of sea urchins,
starfish, abandoned armor of animals
sheltered under your ledges,
in your nooks and crannies,

were crumbling,
           breaking down,
                      diminished,
preparing to leave,
to return to the sea floor,
reabsorbed, renamed.

And I

Knew you would leave me
untethered, soft bellied,
to relearn how to fold in on myself,
to creep warily across the tides of time,
to avoid the Fisherman's Net,
and not drown in the desert air.

## Permanence

Imaginary spaces shimmer,

fade in a moment's breath.

Mind pictures;
burnt grass on an August beach,
a mirage on the road ahead.

Permanence, a forgotten covenant;
a lie told to children
promising security and ever afters.

There are no castles moats to keep fear at arm's length,
no gleaming silvered knights to ward off dreams of loss
that leave behind the ghosts who sustain you in love.

There is only the essence, the strength of who you are
to push past the stone, to remember the harvest moon
that silhouettes pelicans perched on an improbable roof,
atop an improbable house sitting in a field of sand.

## Touching

They told me
*You will touch the heart*
and I saw my hand plunge
into your chest cavity
wriggle through your ribcage
to touch your beating heart.
I put my index finger
on the pulse of you,
tattooed words
only you would understand
that went straight to where poets
place the seat of love.
It found the beat quicken;
you knew I was there
with you
holding
your tired heart in the palm of my hand
while its rhythms sighed in release.

**Just Not Like This**

I don't think I'm angry that you've left me,
I've been left before,

just not like this.

There is only the waxy image
that becomes the shell of you,

but there are no regrets for words left unsaid,
they were all there, flowing out, simple;

"I love you" spoken without tears, over and over,
a hand to stroke your head, close your eyes.

There are loose ends but this is not anger
only the childhood fear that comes

when you are lost in the department store.
I know I will talk to you,

but not with you.

I know I will share my words aloud,
like the child who talked to angels in the dark,

but honey,

I'll never know if you hear them,
Were they good, did you get it?

And in that deep place of mystery
despite my misgivings of all things hidden,

I still will choose to believe
that you would love me enough to lie.

## Shelf

He told me you were on a shelf
surrounded by photographs
of you and him,
maybe even me,
maybe with the grandchildren,

I don't know.

All I am aware of is
I don't want any part of that.

You are not small enough to fit in a box.
You are too big to be pared down to
photographs.

I will not say goodbye
as you drift
on the wind out to sea.

My goodbyes were made
that night right before
the nurse asked if it was time

to open the window.

## The Closet

I gave away parts of you today;
some significant, others not,
some never claimed as your own,
some familiar.
I could see you only as a fading snapshot
wearing them, casual, no big deal.
They no longer had your scent on them;
I checked.
My nose struggled to find you,
buried itself in cotton, linen, raw silk.
Perhaps if your musk was on them,
if I could recall the cologne,
the smell of your hair that brushed the collar,
your sweat lingering in the folds under the armpits
I would have broken my silence,
my lips that held back denials, my clenched teeth
that refused to release a keening of no's
would have burst forth wheeling above my head
dressed in a shroud of black crow feathers.
But today they were only pieces of cloth.
The fabric of you has left the closet
and settled into the fabric of me.

## Drawer

I open a drawer
And my heart falls into it

Recognizes pieces of you
That were left behind

Searches blind
Feels for your essence

In unused razor blades
Wonders if the metal comb

Still holds in its teeth
A piece of your hair

Asks if it should smell it
Try to find your scent

I shake my head no
It beats a slow tattoo

As I swallow it
Back into my chest

As I try to not
Surrender to the brine lump

That forms
At the back of my throat

## Houseplants

I don't understands houseplants
any more than              I understand
oil rigs, advanced math or abandoned cars;

I don't know what to do about them.

They are small enough to live upright in jar lids.
They are arranged, lined up along the sill
                        of my kitchen window
like prisoners about to be shot.

Do I allow them space or clusterthemtogether
so they can,              in their last moments,
talk with each other,
        find mutual bonds in their discomfort?

I offer water and I drown them.
                or wait too long and they shrivel.
Do they know I too am sometimes    drowning,
sometimes              thirsty, parched, brittle

as I try to grasp just how much sustenance
                living things actually need?

## Valley of Fire

You would have loved this;
the red rocks, the monoliths
that speak of how time
metamorphosed into hard rock,
with etched symbols in sunlight,
prayers hidden in crevasses.

I choose to believe they are maps
graved into the rock to guide processions
that petition gods, seek benedictions for water
to drink, cleanse, renew, to baptize the spirit.
Buried with answered prayers,
a river runs under the sands.

It's easy to trust the ancients still visit.
Protected between sunburned rocks
they follow night trails,
feet padding through red dust
escorted by long gone coyote howls,
the shrill of night hawks
the snuffling of mountain lions.

They follow the paths of spectral ancestors;
find clean water that gurgles warm and sweet,
(now thirsty arroyos forgotten by rain).
They do not need to read the walls,
their calloused ghost feet as sure-footed
as the rams they have drawn.

On some nights I imagine
you have been invited
to walk with them.

## A Time When

I have stopped making memories

Memories are for two or more
And they are decorated

With places and ritual things—
The reason you go out to eat

Or prepare a special meal
Or talk about someone you both know

Or sit on the brick stoop
To share the colors of a sunset

I have stopped making memories

There's a blank space in my pages
And no one will know

If it could have been a poem
Or a laugh or heat between the sheets

Because all is now obscured
Silent and imposed

I wait like an un-slept in bed.
That has no scent,

No tranquil dreams or nightmares
To disturb the covers—

I am just there smooth,
Gathering dust for months,

I have stopped making memories

## How silent it is


when you hear the sound of nothing

coursing the chambers of your body
not even the muted tics of time

when the beats of living echo the wall clock
when you almost wish for someone other

a not so silent shadow
a ghost that carries his scent

redolent with ribbons of memory
in old hairbrushes

and cologne no longer used
that sits and waits for no one

on a cluttered shelf
this no-sound amplified

by buzzing flies,
hummingbird chatter

impels me to be aware
reach out in  forced isolation

confident I will someday
hear another voice, hug a friend,

eat and laugh together
leave the masks in a pile

to be sanctified in fire
and memories of lives lost

## After

After you've left
I won't live here anymore.
I'll move away
I'll fire sale our things
and only keep
our dogs,
my studio,
my mother's dishes,
And I'll leave.

I'll go somewhere
where no one knew you.
I won't have to explain
the dichotomy that was you.
I won't have to tell stories
that have nothing to do
with anyone else's lives.

I will live in two large rooms:
one just for me: the studio, a bed;
one just for show.
I will talk to you through walls.
Occasionally I will find you in the mirror.
I will see you
standing beside me
standing behind me
standing pale and ghostly
a chthonic visitor.

After you've left.

**Zing**

Like ropes that have lost their shape,
left outside the shed, unprotected,
their strength gone—

nothing one can use on an icy lake
to pull someone out
who has fallen through.

Like old shoelaces,
when the tips unravel,
contact tenuous at best—

no longer able to tie things together,
all the strands come apart,
some threads thin as filaments.

Zing went the strings of my heart.

## Letting Go

I realized last night that I have stopped
Saying *goodnight my love* to you

I don't know when that happened
It's been awhile

Maybe I have been too tired
Or maybe it just floated away

Absorbed into the ether of my dreams
Last night though it came back to me

And I said it slowly
A little embarrassed to have forgotten

As if something I thought written in marble
Had been chipped away

Like the features of deified ancient rulers
Deliberately marred for eternity

Shamed by jealousy or hubris
But you had no visions of power

And I did not overtake your kingdom
I simply had to let it go

A balloon allowed to fly
Without the onus of a string

## Ash

When I die
dip your fingers
into the ash of me.
Use me to write a poem.
Let it be ours, a collaboration.

Collaborate with me.
Use what is left
to continue the story;
let it sing or howl.
Choose images that speak
for both of us.

Write of the dark red I loved,
the color of placental wine
or the white of stars
or bleached winding sheets.

Lick the tip of your index finger
or wet it in salt water
to scribe with your words
the ones that went unwritten,
the ones I have left behind.

Charlene Stegman Moskal is a Teaching Artist with the Poetry Promise Organization of Las Vegas. She is a visual artist, a performer, a voice for NPR's *Theme and Variations* as well as a writer.

Charlene has been published in *Humana Obscura, Connecticut River Review, The Pensive Journal, Southwestern American Literature, Dash, TAB* and numerous other anthologies, magazines, and online. Her first chapbook is *One Bare Foot,* (Zeitgeist Press, 2018). This chapbook has been written as a memorial to those loved and who have left her life table. She can be found mostly at home in her studio, or with friends in coffee shops and on Zoom workshops sharing writing and stories.